Star Signs for Young Astrologers

Sun Signs, Planets and Houses

Kodi Robinson

Star Signs for Young Astrologers

Sun Signs, Planets and Houses

Written By: Kodi Robinson
Cover & Book Design: Aaron C. Butler

ISBN: 9781967082315 (Paperback)
ISBN: 9781967082322 (eBook)
Library of Congress Control Number: 2025907720

Printed in the United States of America

BookButler Publishing Company
Upper Marlboro, MD 20774

TheBookButler.com

BOOKBUTLER
PUBLISHING COMPANY

Acknowledgments

Thank you, Great Mother Goddess of the Universe, for your infinite spirit. I will continue to discover the mysteries of my existence. Because of you, my evolution continues to blossom. Thank you, ancestors, cosmic elders, and spirit guides, for filling my heart with gratitude. A special thank you to my son Divine, who is a Taurus Sun–you truly are divine. Believe in yourself, always.

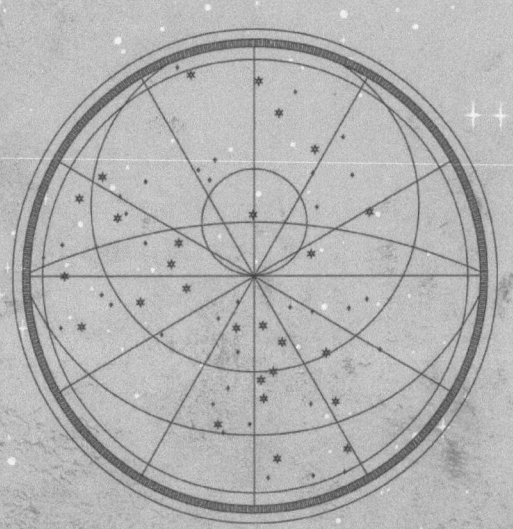

Greetings Cosmic Warrior,

Did you know that the odds of someone having your exact birth chart are one in a million? Your sun sign reveals hidden strengths, life lessons, and the unique energy you bring into the world. The stars have been used for centuries as a cosmic map, guiding people toward self-discovery and purpose. Want to discover what the universe has to say about you?

Hop on board and take a trip to the stars with me! The universe is full of wonder, and astrology helps us understand the magic within it. Our imagination is a powerful tool, guiding us to new ideas and discoveries. When we embrace our creativity, we turn dreams into reality.

Life is as beautiful as you choose to make it—so open your heart, look to the stars, and let your journey begin!

"If you wish for something and it doesn't come true, you didn't wish for it yet."

"When you're happy you don't notice the moon."

- Divine Moon Walker

Table of Contents

What is Astrology? 1

Zodiac, Horoscope, Birth Chart 3

The Zodiac Signs 5

The 4 Elements in Astrology 20

Zodiac Modalities 26

The Planets in Astrology 32

The 12 Astrological Houses 39

The Zodiac as a Whole 48

The Seasons of the Zodiac 49

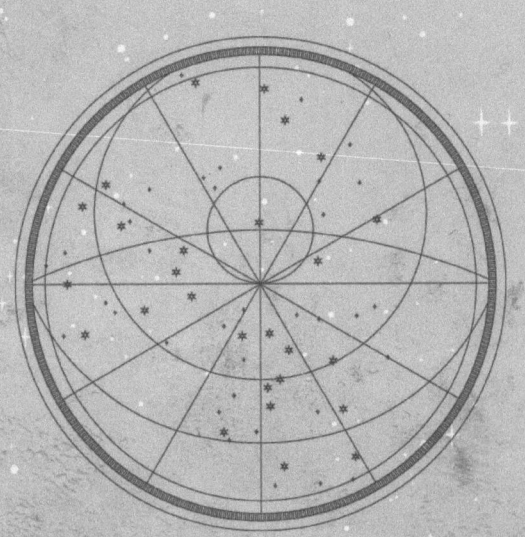

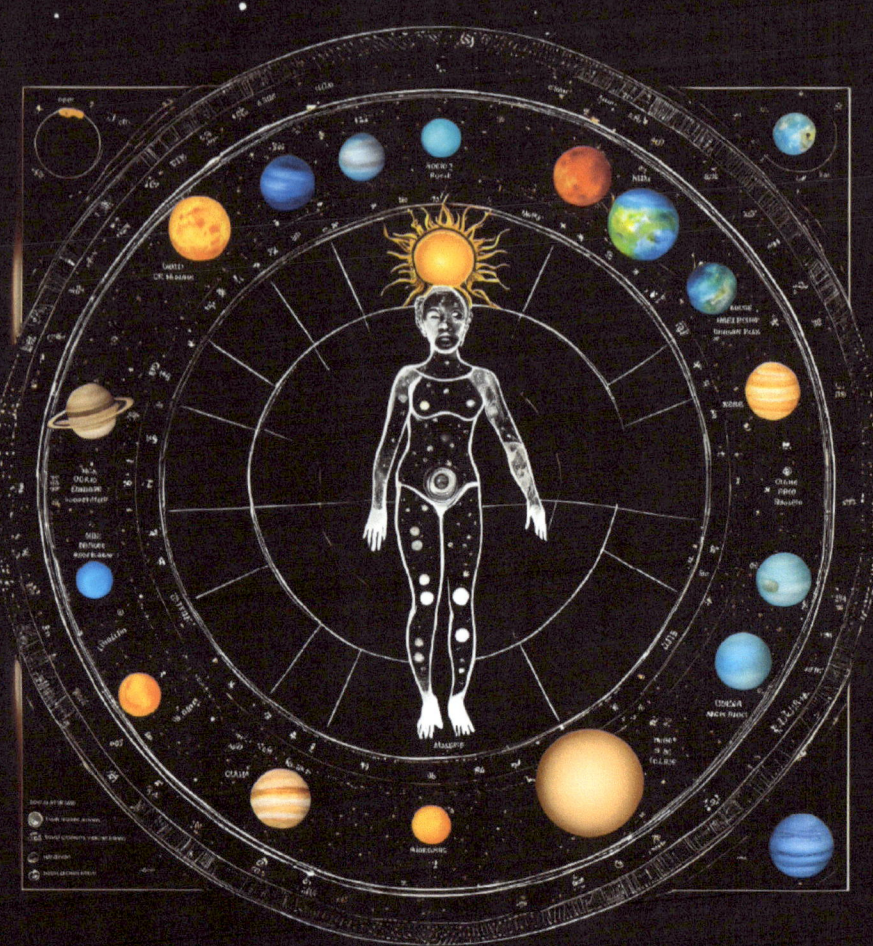

What is Astrology?

Astrology is the study of how cosmic energies influence life on Earth. It is based on the idea that the positions of the planets and stars at the moment of birth shape a person's personality, experiences, and spiritual path. More than just predicting events, astrology is a tool for self-discovery, helping people understand their strengths, challenges, and soul purpose.

For thousands of years, humans have looked to the stars for guidance, using astrology to make sense of their place in the universe. By exploring zodiac signs, planetary movements, and birth charts, astrology provides a roadmap to personal growth and understanding.

Ultimately, astrology is a map of consciousness, guiding us toward greater alignment with the universe and our highest potential. It offers insight into who we are, why we feel the way we do, and how we can navigate life's challenges with clarity and purpose.

Zodiac Horoscope Birth Chart

what is the zodiac?

The zodiac is a belt in the sky where the sun, moon, and planets travel. It is divided into 12 equal sections, known as zodiac signs, each representing different traits, energies, and influences. Your zodiac sign is based on the position of the sun at the moment of your birth.

what is a horoscope?

A horoscope is a chart that shows the positions of the planets and zodiac signs at a specific moment in time, like the instant you were born. Astrologers use horoscopes to interpret personality traits, strengths, challenges, and life opportunities. Each person's horoscope is unique, like a cosmic fingerprint.

what is a birth chart?

A birth chart, also known as a natal chart, is a detailed map of where the planets, moon, and sun were positioned at the exact moment of your birth. It serves as a personal guide, helping you understand your strengths, challenges, and purpose in life. Each chart is divided into 12 sections, called houses, which represent different areas of life.

The Zodiac Signs

Each zodiac sign carries a unique energy shaped by its element, modality, ruling planet, and core traits. These signs influence how we express ourselves, interact with others, and navigate life's journey. The season of a sign's arrival also plays a role in its essence–spring signs bring renewal, summer signs radiate growth, autumn signs reflect transformation, and winter signs embody wisdom and endurance.

The following in-depth exploration of each zodiac sign, offers insight into its strengths, challenges, and guiding affirmation.

ARIES
(MARCH 21 – APRIL 19) – THE RAM

"I AM"

Element: Fire | **Modality:** Cardinal | **Ruling Planet:** Mars
Body Part: Head & Face | **Colors:** Red, Orange
Lucky Stones: Diamond, Ruby, Red Jasper, Amethyst

A spark of energy ignites with Aries, the first sign of the zodiac. Born to lead, initiate, and take bold action, Aries thrives in new beginnings. Their natural bravery pushes them to chase after their goals without hesitation. However, their challenge is to balance impulsiveness with wisdom, learning to direct their energy toward a higher purpose rather than personal gain. When they evolve beyond self-interest, Aries becomes a powerful force for change and inspiration.

Affirmation: "I embrace my fearless nature, channeling my energy into bold and meaningful action."

TAURUS
(APRIL 20 – MAY 20) – THE BULL

"I HAVE"

Element: Earth | **Modality:** Fixed | **Ruling Planet:** Venus
Body Part: Neck | **Colors:** Pink, Bright Green
Lucky Stones: Emerald, Sapphire, Turquoise

With deep roots in the physical world, Taurus finds peace and value in stability, patience, and the beauty of life. Drawn to comfort and security, they excel at building lasting foundations. However, their lesson is to understand that true wealth is not material, but spiritual. When they release attachment to possessions and embrace inner abundance, Taurus teaches others how to live with balance, gratitude, and unshakable inner peace.

Affirmation: "I cultivate abundance and security, embracing the beauty of life's simple pleasures."

GEMINI
(MAY 21 – JUNE 20) – THE TWINS

"I THINK"

Element: Air | **Modality:** Mutable | **Ruling Planet:** Mercury
Body Part: Arms | **Colors:** Yellow
Lucky Stones: Opal, Agate, Pearl, Moonstone

Gemini is a seeker of knowledge, connection, and intellectual discovery. Quick-witted and expressive, they thrive on conversation and exchanging ideas. Their challenge is to quiet the mind and focus on what truly matters, learning to use their words not just to communicate, but to uplift and inspire. When they master this, Gemini becomes a powerful messenger of wisdom and truth.

Affirmation: "I embrace my curiosity and express myself with clarity and confidence."

CANCER
(JUNE 21 – JULY 22) – THE CRAB

"I FEEL"

Element: Water | **Modality:** Cardinal
Ruling Planet: Moon | **Body Part:** Chest
Colors: Grey, Silver, White
Lucky Stones: Citrine, Rose Quartz, Emerald

Emotional depth and intuition define Cancer, the protector of the zodiac. They are deeply connected to home, family, and the past, carrying a natural ability to nurture and care for others. However, their lesson is to let go of emotional wounds and trust their inner strength. When they learn to offer love freely without becoming overly attached, Cancer's heart radiates unconditional love and emotional security.

Affirmation: "I honor my emotions and create a safe, loving space for myself and others."

LEO

(JULY 23 – AUGUST 22) – THE LION

"I WILL"

Element: Fire | **Modality:** Fixed | **Ruling Planet:** Sun
Body Part: Heart | **Colors:** Red, Yellow, Orange
Lucky Stones: Ruby, Carnelian, Diamond, Peridot

Born to shine, Leo radiates confidence, creativity, and passion. They embrace the spotlight, thriving when they express themselves and inspire others. However, their challenge is to balance self-importance with humility, learning to use their natural gifts not for personal recognition, but for the greater good. When they shift from seeking attention to spreading light, Leo becomes a source of inspiration and strength for others.

Affirmation: "I lead with confidence and inspire others through my passion and kindness."

11

VIRGO
(AUGUST 23 – SEPTEMBER 22) – THE MAIDEN

"I ANALYZE"

Element: Earth | **Modality:** Mutable

Ruling Planet: Mercury | **Body Part:** Digestive System

Colors: White, Brown, Green

Lucky Stones: Topaz, Moss Agate, Sapphire

With a mind for service, organization, and improvement, Virgo is always looking for ways to make things better. Their keen eye for detail helps them bring order to chaos, but they must learn to release perfectionism and trust that their efforts are enough. When they offer help without expectation and find joy in the process, Virgo becomes a humble healer and a source of wisdom for those in need.

Affirmation: "I embrace my gifts of precision and service, knowing that growth is a journey."

LIBRA
(SEPTEMBER 23 – OCTOBER 22) – THE SCALES

"I BALANCE"

Element: Air | **Modality:** Cardinal | **Ruling Planet:** Venus
Body Part: Kidneys | **Colors:** Pink
Lucky Stones: Quartz, Opal, Aquamarine, Lapis Lazuli

Life is a dance of balance and relationships for Libra, who seeks peace, fairness, and beauty in all things. Naturally diplomatic, they bring people together and foster harmony. However, their challenge is to avoid losing themselves in the desire to please others. When they learn to balance their own needs with the needs of others, Libra becomes a source of true partnership and understanding.

Affirmation: "I embrace balance and beauty, making choices that align with my highest good."

SCORPIO
(OCTOBER 23 – NOVEMBER 22) – THE SCORPION

"I DESIRE"

Element: Water | **Modality:** Fixed

Ruling Planet: Pluto (Ancient Ruler: Mars)

Body Part: Reproductive System, Hips

Colors: Black, Violet, Deep Red

Lucky Stones: Jade, Ruby, Coral, Carnelian

Scorpio delves into the depths of emotions, transformation, and truth. Fearless in the face of change, they embrace life's mysteries and challenges. However, their lesson is to release control and trust the process of rebirth. When they move beyond fear and surrender to transformation, Scorpio becomes a powerful healer and a guiding light for deep soul evolution.

Affirmation: "I embrace transformation, allowing my passions to guide me toward growth and wisdom."

SAGITTARIUS
(NOVEMBER 23 – DECEMBER 21) – THE ARCHER

"I SEE"

Element: Fire | **Modality:** Mutable | **Ruling Planet:** Jupiter
Body Part: Thighs, Hips | **Colors:** Blue, Purple, Yellow
Lucky Stones: Sapphire, Diamond, Lapis Lazuli, Turquoise

With a thirst for adventure, wisdom, and higher purpose, Sagittarius is always searching for deeper meaning. They explore the world through travel, philosophy, and experience, but must learn to turn their quest for truth inward, not just outward. When they ground their expansive energy in spiritual wisdom, Sagittarius becomes a teacher who inspires others to seek their own truth.

Affirmation: "I explore the world with an open heart and embrace the wisdom that every journey brings."

CAPRICORN
(DECEMBER 22 – JANUARY 19) – THE GOAT

"I USE"

Element: Earth | **Modality:** Cardinal
Ruling Planet: Saturn | **Body Part:** Knees, Teeth, Bones
Colors: Brown, Black, Blue
Lucky Stones: Amber, Onyx, Sapphire, Quartz

Hardworking and ambitious, Capricorn is focused on discipline, structure, and achieving lasting success. They are determined to climb the highest mountains, but must learn that true success comes from spiritual growth, not just material accomplishments. When they align their ambition with a higher purpose, Capricorn becomes a wise leader who uplifts others through strength and integrity.

Affirmation: "I build my future with patience and dedication, knowing that success is a journey."

AQUARIUS
(JANUARY 20 – FEBRUARY 18) – THE WATER BEARER

"I KNOW"

Element: Air | **Modality:** Fixed

Ruling Planet: Uranus (Ancient Ruler: Saturn)

Body Part: Ankles, Circulatory System

Colors: Green, Black, Blue

Lucky Stones: Amber, Onyx, Zircon

Aquarius thrives in the realm of innovation, progress, and humanitarianism. Always ahead of their time, they bring fresh ideas and unconventional thinking. However, their challenge is to ground their visions into reality and use their gifts for the collective good. When they channel their creativity into meaningful action, Aquarius becomes a visionary leader who inspires transformation in the world.

Affirmation: "I honor my unique perspective and use my vision to inspire positive change."

PISCES
(FEBRUARY 19 – MARCH 20) – THE FISH

"I BELIEVE"

Element: Water **| Modality: Mutable**
Ruling Planet: Neptune (Ancient Ruler: Jupiter)
Body Part: Feet **| Colors:** Purple, Grey, Blue
Lucky Stones: Pink Coral, Turquoise, Aquamarine

Deeply sensitive and intuitive, Pisces feels the energy of the universe and connects with the unseen. They hold immense compassion and creativity, but must learn to release illusions and trust in their inner guidance. When they embrace their spiritual gifts and serve as a beacon of love, Pisces becomes a compassionate healer, helping others awaken to divine truth.

Affirmation: "I trust my intuition and embrace the beauty of my imagination."

The 4 Elements in Astrology

FIRE, EARTH, AIR, AND WATER

In astrology, the four elements serve as the foundation of the zodiac, shaping the personality traits and energies of each sign. These elements represent the fundamental forces of nature and influence how we think, feel, and interact with the world. Understanding the elements helps us see patterns in our behaviors, relationships, and spiritual journeys. By recognizing the element associated with our zodiac sign, we gain deeper insight into our natural strengths, challenges, and ways of expressing ourselves.

Each zodiac sign belongs to one of these four elements, sharing key characteristics with others in the same category. Fire signs bring passion, Earth signs provide stability, Air signs offer intellect, and Water signs nurture deep emotions. While each sign expresses its element uniquely, the element itself creates an underlying theme that influences how that sign interacts with life.

FIRE SIGNS

ARIES, LEO, SAGITTARIUS

THE ENERGY OF PASSION AND ACTION

Fire is the element of energy, drive, and enthusiasm. It represents passion, courage, creativity, and inspiration. Fire signs are known for their boldness, determination, and ability to take action. They are natural leaders, driven by excitement and a desire to forge new paths. Like a flame, they burn brightly and bring warmth to those around them, but they can also become overwhelming if not balanced.

Aries, Leo, and Sagittarius express fire in different ways. Aries is the spark, initiating new ideas and boldly stepping into challenges. Leo is the steady flame, radiating confidence and leadership. Sagittarius is the wildfire, seeking adventure, truth, and freedom. Fire signs must learn to temper their intensity with patience and mindfulness, ensuring that their energy is directed toward meaningful pursuits.

Affirmation: "I embrace my passion and creativity, using my energy to inspire and uplift others."

WATER SIGNS

CANCER, SCORPIO, PISCES

THE ENERGY OF EMOTION AND INTUITION

Water represents deep emotions, intuition, healing, and spirituality. It is the element of the subconscious, flowing through our dreams, instincts, and inner wisdom. Water signs are deeply connected to their feelings and the emotions of others, making them highly empathetic and nurturing. They remind us of the power of emotional intelligence and the importance of listening to our inner voice.

Cancer, Scorpio, and Pisces express water energy in unique ways. Cancer is the gentle stream, protective and nurturing, providing emotional security. Scorpio is the powerful ocean, intense and transformative, diving into life's deepest mysteries. Pisces is the mystical mist, dreamy and imaginative, bridging the physical world with the spiritual. Water signs must learn to balance their emotions with logic, ensuring that their deep sensitivity does not lead to overwhelm.

Affirmation: "I trust my intuition and embrace the depth of my emotions as a source of strength."

AIR SIGNS

GEMINI, LIBRA, AQUARIUS

THE ENERGY OF THOUGHT AND COMMUNICATION

Air represents intellect, curiosity, communication, and innovation. It is the element of ideas, movement, and social connection, governing how we think, speak, and interact with the world. Air signs thrive on exchanging knowledge, fostering new perspectives, and seeking truth. They are visionaries, constantly exploring possibilities and pushing boundaries.

Gemini, Libra, and Aquarius each embody air in a distinct way. Gemini is the breeze, quick-witted, adaptable, and always seeking new information. Libra is the balanced wind, harmonizing relationships and striving for fairness and beauty. Aquarius is the storm, bringing revolutionary ideas and challenging the status quo. Air signs must be mindful of staying grounded, as their tendency to live in the realm of thought can sometimes detach them from their emotions and physical reality.

Affirmation: "I welcome new ideas and perspectives, using my voice to bring wisdom and connection to the world."

EARTH SIGNS

TAURUS, VIRGO, CAPRICORN

THE ENERGY OF STABILITY AND GROWTH

Earth represents grounding, reliability, patience, and practicality. It is the element of foundation and endurance, providing structure and stability in both the physical and emotional realms. Earth signs are deeply connected to the material world, valuing hard work, security, and tangible results. They are the builders and nurturers, creating lasting legacies through their dedication and perseverance.

Taurus, Virgo, and Capricorn express earth energy uniquely. Taurus is the fertile soil, embracing comfort, beauty, and a deep connection to nature. Virgo is the cultivator, focusing on detail, refinement, and self-improvement. Capricorn is the mountain, steadily climbing toward success and long-term goals. Earth signs must be mindful not to become too rigid or overly focused on material gain, remembering that growth also requires adaptability.

Affirmation: "I am grounded, strong, and capable of building a stable and fulfilling life."

Balancing the Elements in Our Lives
△ ▽ △ ▽

While each of us has a dominant element based on our birth chart, we all possess aspects of Fire, Earth, Air, and Water within us. Understanding how these elements interact helps us find balance. Too much fire can lead to impulsiveness, while too little can result in a lack of motivation. Excess earth may create stubbornness, while a lack of it can lead to instability. An abundance of air might cause overthinking, while too little may hinder communication. Too much water can result in emotional overwhelm, while too little might make it difficult to connect with feelings.

By recognizing these elements within ourselves, we can nurture areas that need more balance and appreciate the strengths we naturally possess. Each element plays a crucial role in shaping who we are and how we navigate the world.

Affirmation: "I honor the balance of Fire, Earth, Air, and Water within me, embracing my strengths and learning from each element's wisdom."

ZODIAC MODALITIES

 Cardinal

ARIES CANCER LIBRA CAPRICORN

This modality marks the beginning of each season. Cardinal signs are active and ambitious!

 **Fixed**

TAURUS LEO SCORPIO AQUARIUS

This modality holds each season in place. Fixed signs are steady and determined!

 Mutable

GEMINI VIRGO SAGITTARIUS PISCES

This modality changes each season to the next. Mutable signs are flexible and imaginative!

The 3 Modalities in Astrology
CARDINAL, FIXED, AND MUTABLE

In astrology, the three modalities represent how each zodiac sign interacts with the world. represent different ways the soul expresses its energy and purpose. These modalities go beyond personality traits and show how a soul moves through spiritual growth and service. Each modality contains four zodiac signs, one from each element, creating a balance between fire, earth, air, and water.

Understanding the modalities helps us see how different signs initiate, sustain, or adapt to life's experiences. Whether you are a natural leader, a determined builder, or a flexible thinker, your modality influences how you navigate challenges and opportunities.

CARDINAL MODALITY — THE INITIATORS OF DIVINE WILL

Cardinal signs are the pioneers of the zodiac, bringing fresh energy and new beginnings. They mark the start of each season:

- Aries begins spring
- Cancer starts summer
- Libra ushers in autumn
- Capricorn announces winter

These signs represent the energy of initiation, leadership, and the birth of new spiritual ideas. Souls influenced by this modality are natural pioneers, often bringing in higher wisdom or new ways of thinking to help humanity evolve. These individuals are called to act as channels for divine will, setting powerful energies into motion. However, they must learn to act with higher guidance rather than personal ambition.

Affirmation: "I embrace new beginnings with confidence and courage, using my energy to inspire and lead."

FIXED MODALITY – THE ANCHORS OF SPIRITUAL POWER

Fixed signs are the steady, determined forces of the zodiac. They occur in the middle of each season, representing stability and persistence. These signs don't just start things–they see them through to completion.

- Taurus sustains the growth of spring
- Leo fuels the heat of summer
- Scorpio deepens the intensity of autumn
- Aquarius carries the vision of winter

These signs hold and stabilize energy, ensuring that divine wisdom is grounded and sustained. Souls influenced by this modality are here to develop inner strength, perseverance, and mastery over their thoughts and emotions.

They act as spiritual anchors, keeping divine truth steady even when the outer world is chaotic. Their challenge is to avoid stubbornness and be open to evolution while maintaining spiritual integrity.

Affirmation: "I am strong and determined. My focus and dedication allow me to build lasting success."

MUTABLE MODALITY – THE MESSENGERS OF LIGHT

Mutable signs are the flexible, adaptable, and versatile thinkers of the zodiac. They mark the end of each season, preparing for transition and change.

- Gemini shifts spring into summer
- Virgo refines summer into autumn
- Sagittarius expands autumn into winter
- Pisces softens winter into spring

These signs represent the ability to adapt, learn, and transmit spiritual knowledge. Souls influenced by this modality are here to bridge different dimensions of consciousness, making complex truths accessible to others. They are often teachers, healers, or messengers, moving between realms to bring guidance and healing. Their challenge is to remain focused and not become scattered or lost in illusion.

Affirmation: "I welcome change and growth, trusting in my ability to adapt and thrive."

Finding Balance Among the Modalities

While each person has a dominant modality based on their birth chart, we all benefit from understanding and balancing these energies.

- Cardinal energy inspires action, but needs follow-through.
- Fixed energy builds stability, but benefits from openness to change.
- Mutable energy encourages adaptability, but needs grounding.

By recognizing these patterns within ourselves, we can harness our strengths and grow in areas where we seek balance. Whether we are leading, building, or adapting, the modalities remind us that each stage of life is essential to personal growth.

Affirmation: "I honor the balance of initiation, stability, and adaptability within me, embracing each stage of my journey."

31

The Planets in Astrology

In astrology, each planet represents a different aspect of our personality, soul journey, and spiritual evolution. They influence how we think, feel, act, and grow, guiding us toward self-awareness and transformation. They are seen as teachers, offering wisdom that helps us align with our highest potential.

It's important to note that while astrology refers to all celestial bodies as "planets," the Sun and the Moon are actually luminaries, not planets. They hold a special place in astrology, representing the core of our being and emotional depth.

THE SUN
CORE PURPOSE & IDENTITY

The Sun represents your soul's essence, purpose, and identity. It is the center of your birth chart, showing where you are meant to grow and shine in life. The Sun's energy encourages you to develop confidence, self-awareness, and leadership. It represents the higher self and the journey of self-realization. *Note: The Sun is a luminary, not a planet.*

Guiding Question: How can I step fully into my purpose and radiate my light?

THE MOON
EMOTIONS & INTUITION

The Moon governs your emotions, intuitive nature, and subconscious patterns. It reflects past life experiences and deep soul memories, teaching you how to heal emotional wounds and move beyond limiting beliefs. In astrology, the Moon represents the soul's karmic lessons and the path to inner emotional wisdom. *Note: The Moon is also a luminary, not a planet.*

Guiding Question: What emotions and patterns do I need to heal to move forward?

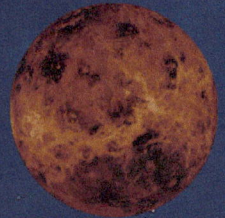

MERCURY
COMMUNICATION & MIND

Mercury rules thinking, communication, and learning. It influences how we process information, express ideas, and make decisions. In astrology, Mercury represents the wisdom gained through knowledge and the ability to use the mind as a tool for higher understanding.

Guiding Question: How can I use my voice and thoughts to share wisdom and truth?

VENUS
LOVE & HARMONY

Venus governs love, beauty, relationships, and personal values. It teaches us about harmony, attraction, and emotional balance. On a deeper level, Venus in astrology shows how to integrate love with spiritual wisdom, allowing relationships to become paths of personal and soul growth.

Guiding Question: How can I cultivate love that nurtures my soul and others?

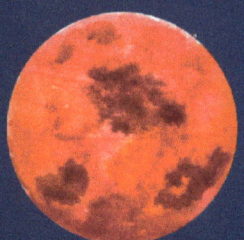

MARS
ACTION & STRENGTH

Mars represents action, energy, and ambition. It fuels our passions and gives us the drive to go after what we desire. In astrology, Mars teaches us how to use strength and willpower for spiritual growth, encouraging us to turn challenges into opportunities for transformation.

Guiding Question: How can I channel my energy into meaningful and purposeful action?

JUPITER
EXPANSION & HIGHER KNOWLEDGE

Jupiter is the planet of wisdom, growth, and abundance. It encourages exploration, both physically (through travel) and intellectually (through higher learning). Jupiter represents the understanding of universal laws and the soul's journey toward enlightenment.

Guiding Question: What new knowledge or experiences will help me grow spiritually?

SATURN
DISCIPLINE & LIFE LESSONS

Saturn is the great teacher of discipline, responsibility, and structure. It brings challenges that test our patience and endurance, but these trials ultimately lead to spiritual strength. Saturn represents karmic lessons and the mastery of life's obstacles.

Guiding Question: What challenges in my life are teaching me to be stronger and wiser?

URANUS
INNOVATION & CHANGE

Uranus is the planet of sudden breakthroughs, originality, and freedom. It urges us to break away from old patterns and embrace new perspectives. In astrology, Uranus helps the soul evolve by shattering outdated beliefs and awakening higher consciousness.

Guiding Question: How can I embrace change and step into my most authentic self?

NEPTUNE
INTUITION & SPIRITUAL AWAKENING

Neptune rules dreams, intuition, and spirituality. It connects us to the unseen realms, encouraging imagination, creativity, and deep compassion. Neptune teaches us to trust in the flow of the universe and develop our spiritual gifts.

Guiding Question: How can I trust my intuition and connect with my higher self?

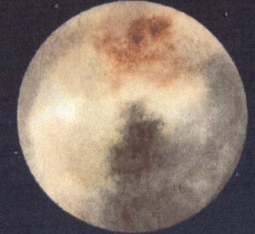

PLUTO
TRANSFORMATION & REBIRTH

Pluto is the planet of deep transformation, power, and rebirth. It helps us shed old identities, face our fears, and emerge stronger. In astrology, Pluto represents soul evolution and the process of spiritual renewal.

Guiding Question: What do I need to release in order to step into my highest self?

UNDERSTANDING THE PLANETS

Each planet plays a role in shaping your journey, from how you express yourself to how you learn and grow. By exploring their influence in your birth chart, you can gain profound insight into your soul's path and purpose.

Affirmation: "I align with the wisdom of the planets, using their guidance to evolve and fulfill my highest potential."

Birth Chart

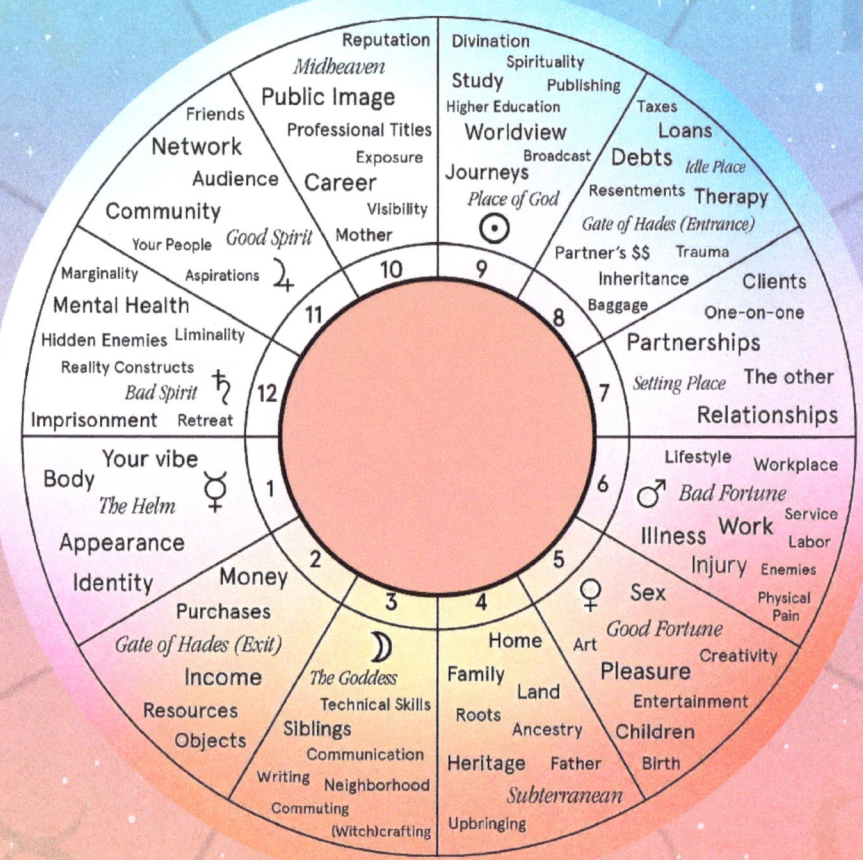

The 12 astrological houses wheel, reading clockwise from house 10 at the top:

House 10: Reputation, Midheaven, Public Image, Professional Titles, Exposure, Career, Visibility, Mother

House 9: Divination, Spirituality, Study, Publishing, Higher Education, Worldview, Broadcast, Journeys, Place of God ☉

House 8: Taxes, Loans, Debts, Idle Place, Resentments, Therapy, Gate of Hades (Entrance), Partner's $$, Trauma, Inheritance, Baggage

House 7: Clients, One-on-one, Partnerships, The other, Setting Place, Relationships

House 6: Lifestyle, Workplace, ♂ Bad Fortune, Service, Illness, Work, Labor, Injury, Enemies, Physical Pain

House 5: Sex ♀, Good Fortune, Art, Creativity, Pleasure, Entertainment, Children, Birth

House 4: Home, Family, Land, Roots, Ancestry, Heritage, Father, Subterranean, Upbringing

House 3: Gate of Hades (Exit), Money, Purchases, Income, Resources, Objects, ☽ The Goddess, Technical Skills, Siblings, Communication, Writing, Neighborhood, Commuting, (Witch)crafting

House 2: Money, Purchases, Income, Resources, Objects

House 1: Your vibe, Body, The Helm ☿, Appearance, Identity

House 12: Mental Health, Hidden Enemies, Liminality, Reality Constructs, Bad Spirit ♄, Imprisonment, Retreat

House 11: Friends, Network, Audience, Community, Your People, Good Spirit ♃, Marginality, Aspirations

THE 12 ASTROLOGICAL HOUSES

Each of the 12 houses in astrology represents a different area of life, shaping our experiences, personal growth, and soul's journey. They provide insight into who we are, how we connect with others, and the lessons we are meant to learn. These houses act as a spiritual blueprint, guiding us toward self-discovery and deeper understanding.

 The House of Self

Who are you at your core? The First House holds the answer. As the starting point of your soul's journey, it shapes your identity, personal expression, and the way you present yourself to the world. Learning to embrace this house helps you develop confidence, independence, and a strong sense of self. When you understand it, you become a leader by simply being yourself.

Affirmation: "I am always discovering how uniquely wonderful I am. By embracing my true self, I shine with confidence and authenticity."

2 The House of Values & Abundance

What truly matters to you? The Second House asks you to reflect on your values, self-worth, and relationship with abundance. While often associated with money and material possessions, this house teaches that real wealth comes from within. It encourages you to recognize the power of gratitude, generosity, and inner security. When you master this house, you understand that your greatest treasure is your spirit, not your wallet.

Affirmation: "I was born abundant; I am a divine magnet for prosperity. My worth is not measured by what I own but by the richness of my spirit."

3 The House of Communication & Learning

Words hold power, and the Third House teaches you how to use them wisely. This house governs communication, learning, and self-expression, shaping the way you think and share ideas with the world. More than just absorbing facts, it encourages you to seek deeper truths and meaningful connections. Listening with your heart and speaking with intention allows your words to bring healing and knowledge to others.

41

Affirmation: "I am safe to express my thoughts truthfully and politely. My voice matters, and I communicate with clarity and confidence."

 ## The House of Home & Family

Where do you feel most at home? The Fourth House reminds you that true security comes not from a place, but from within. Representing your roots, family, and emotional foundation, this house helps you release fear and embrace the safety of your inner world. It also connects you to past lives and deep soul memories. When you master this house, you carry peace within you, no matter where you go.

Affirmation: "I love myself, therefore I respect my parents and honor my ancestors. Their wisdom and love have helped shape me into the person I am today."

 ## The House of Creativity & Joy

How do you express the light within you? The Fifth House inspires joy, creativity, and self-expression, teaching you that happiness is found in sharing your gifts with the world. Whether through art, play, or acts of love, this house encourages you to create something meaningful. When you stop seeking approval and instead focus on authentic self-expression, your joy becomes a guiding light for others.

Affirmation: "I decide to be me. I approve of myself as I am now, leaving room for growth. My creativity and joy are limitless."

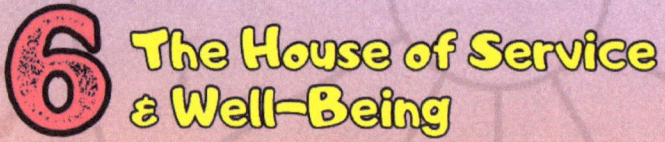

6 The House of Service & Well-Being

How do you show up for yourself and others? The Sixth House teaches that purpose is found in service and daily acts of devotion. Whether through work, health, or simple routines, this house reminds you that even small actions carry deep meaning. Taking care of your body, mind, and spirit ensures you can better support the world around you. When you master this house, your life becomes an offering of love and healing.

Affirmation: "My body is my temple; I nurture it with high-vibrational, nutritional fuel to stay happy and healthy. I honor my well-being."

7 The House of Relationships & Partnerships

Who do you attract into your life? The Seventh House reveals that every relationship serves as a mirror, reflecting back lessons about yourself. Instead of looking for someone to complete you, this house teaches that true love begins within. When you build relationships based on mutual growth and understanding, they become a path to wisdom, healing, and transformation.

Affirmation: "I only attract loving individuals in my world, for they are a mirror of who I am. My relationships are built on love, respect, and harmony."

8 The House of Transformation

What parts of yourself must you let go of to grow? The Eighth House is a place of deep transformation, rebirth, and personal power. Just like a butterfly emerging from a cocoon, this house encourages you to release fears, embrace change, and step into your true potential. It is also connected to life's greatest mysteries, such as energy, intuition, and spiritual evolution.

Affirmation: "I rejoice in others' good fortune. There is plenty for everyone, including me. Transformation leads me to a stronger and wiser self."

9 The House of Wisdom & Exploration

What is your truth? The Ninth House guides you toward higher learning, spiritual growth, and the pursuit of wisdom. It teaches that true knowledge doesn't just come from books–it comes from experience, open-mindedness, and deep exploration. Whether through travel, education, or philosophical inquiry, this house encourages you to expand your mind and embrace the unknown.

Affirmation: "I am learning and growing every day. The world is my classroom, and wisdom is my greatest treasure."

10 The House of Purpose & Legacy

What impact will you leave on the world? The Tenth House represents your life's mission, career, and the mark you make on society. Success isn't about fame or wealth–it's about using your talents to serve a greater purpose. This house helps you step into leadership by leading with integrity, responsibility, and authenticity.

Affirmation: "Success is truly liking myself, what I do, and how I do it. I am building a future filled with purpose and integrity."

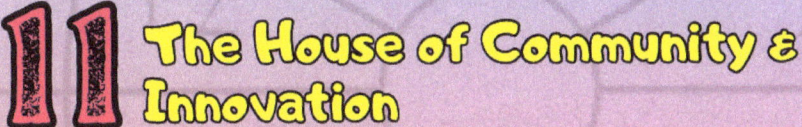 11 The House of Community & Innovation

How do you contribute to something bigger than yourself? The Eleventh House is about friendships, social movements, and collective progress. It teaches that change is most powerful when people come together for a common cause. Whether through activism, humanitarian efforts, or creative collaboration, this house encourages you to align with like-minded souls to build a better future.

Affirmation: "The world is a better place because I'm in it. My dreams uplift not only me but those around me."

12 The House of Spirituality & Inner Growth

What happens when you surrender to the unknown? The Twelfth House is a place of spiritual connection, deep healing, and the release of ego. It reminds you that you are more than just an individual–you are a soul, connected to the infinite wisdom of the universe. When you embrace the mysteries of life, you find peace in knowing that everything is unfolding as it should.

Affirmation: "If I know better, I do better. My intuition is my guide, leading me toward enlightenment and peace."

Understanding the Houses

Each house represents a different lesson, experience, and opportunity for growth. By exploring them in your birth chart, you can navigate life with greater clarity, awareness, and purpose.

Affirmation: "I honor the wisdom of the houses, embracing the journey of self-discovery and transformation."

THE ZODIAC AS A WHOLE

Each zodiac sign holds a unique energy and wisdom, guiding us through life's journey. As we grow, we learn to embrace the highest expression of our sign, discovering our strengths, challenges, and purpose. Together, the zodiac weaves a beautiful balance, with each sign playing a vital role in the universe's grand design.

As a young astrologer, you have the power to unlock the secrets of the stars. By exploring your sign, you gain deeper insight into who you are, how you connect with others, and the bigger picture of life itself. Astrology is more than just learning about the zodiac—it's a journey of self-discovery, growth, and cosmic connection. Astrology is the language of the universe and the rhythm of your soul—a cosmic melody that guides your journey. Listen to its song, embrace its wisdom, and let's dance with the stars! Let them guide you on an exciting adventure of knowledge, wonder, and self-discovery!

Affirmation: "I honor the wisdom of the stars, embracing my journey with awareness and purpose."

SEASONS OF THE ZODIAC:
THE CYCLE OF LIFE AND GROWTH

The seasons of the year align with the seasons of life, reflecting different stages of personal growth and transformation. Just as nature shifts through cycles of renewal, expansion, reflection, and rest, so do we. Each zodiac sign carries the essence of the season in which it occurs, shaping its energy, purpose, and contribution to the greater whole.

SPRING
ARIES, TAURUS, GEMINI
BIRTH & RENEWAL

Spring represents new beginnings, fresh energy, and the excitement of possibility. Like birth and early childhood, this season is full of curiosity, enthusiasm, and the drive to explore. Aries, as the first sign of the zodiac, initiates this season with boldness and a pioneering spirit. Taurus follows, bringing stability and patience to nurture new growth. Gemini completes the season with curiosity and adaptability, encouraging learning and communication.

SUMMER

CANCER, LEO, VIRGO
YOUTH & EXPANSION

Summer embodies vitality, passion, and the blossoming of personal identity. Like youth, this season is about self-expression, confidence, and connection. Cancer nurtures emotional depth and strengthens bonds with family and loved ones. Leo steps into the spotlight, radiating creativity, leadership, and joy. Virgo refines the details, encouraging self-improvement and the pursuit of purpose through dedication and service.

AUTUMN

LIBRA, SCORPIO, SAGITTARIUS
ADULTHOOD & TRANSFORMATION

Autumn symbolizes change, maturity, and the wisdom gained through experience. Just as adulthood brings a deeper understanding of relationships, personal power, and truth, this season reflects a period of balance and transformation. Libra begins the season by seeking harmony and justice, fostering meaningful relationships. Scorpio follows, delving into the depths of self-discovery and embracing transformation. Sagittarius concludes the season with an adventurous spirit, expanding knowledge and seeking wisdom through exploration.

WINTER
CAPRICORN, AQUARIUS, PISCES
ELDERHOOD & WISDOM

Winter represents introspection, reflection, and the culmination of life's lessons. Like elderhood, this season calls for patience, wisdom, and spiritual awareness. Capricorn builds a lasting legacy, demonstrating discipline and perseverance. Aquarius innovates, bringing visionary ideas and progress for the future. Pisces embraces the unseen, merging intuition, creativity, and universal connection to complete the cycle before it begins again in Aries.

Farewell Cosmic Warrior and remember...

You are part of something vast, beautiful, and full of wisdom. Astrology is more than just studying the stars — it's a journey of self-discovery, growth, and connection. The universe is alive with rhythms and patterns, guiding you through the ever-changing cycles of life. By exploring your zodiac sign, element, modality, and planetary influences, you unlock the wisdom of the cosmos and gain a deeper understanding of who you are and the path you are meant to follow.

Each sign carries a unique lesson, and together, they create a beautiful balance. Fire signs remind you to live with passion and courage. Earth signs ground you in stability and perseverance. Air signs inspire you to think, learn, and connect. Water signs teach you the power of emotions and intuition. By embracing these energies, you become part of the greater cosmic dance, growing and evolving with the universe itself.

Astrology also helps you understand the people around you. By recognizing the strengths and challenges of each sign, you learn to appreciate differences, build deeper connections, and navigate life's relationships with compassion and wisdom.

Above all, astrology is a reminder that you are part of something grand. Just as the stars move through their cycles, so do you—learning, evolving, and discovering new possibilities along the way. The universe is always speaking to you. Whenever you need guidance, simply look up—the stars will always be there to light your path.

Trust in your journey, embrace the wisdom of the cosmos, and let your light shine bright. The stars are always there to guide you—whenever you need direction, simply look up.

Affirmation: "I am one with the universe flowing in harmony with the stars and planets. My soul reflects the wisdom of the cosmos and I trust the divine timing of my journey. I embrace my purpose, my power, and my infinite connection to all that is."

About the Author

Kodi Robinson is an astrologer and storyteller who believes that astrology is a powerful tool for self-discovery. She has always been curious about life's big questions... What is life? Why are we here? What shapes our reality? – and has found astrology to be a guiding light in understanding our purpose and place in the universe.

From a young age, Kodi's love for writing, speaking, and performing fueled her passion for storytelling. Whether through the written word, the stage, or the screen, she uses creativity to connect with others and share meaningful ideas.

In Star Signs for Young Astrologers, Kodi invites young readers on a journey to discover their unique talents, embrace who they are, and unlock the power within themselves. She believes the key to happiness and success lies in truly knowing and loving yourself—and that the stars can help light the way.